THE NATIVITY
According to Mommy

By Carole "Lisa Lynn" Gilbert

But an angel said to them, "Do not be afraid. I bring you good news of great joy that will be for all the people. Today in the town of David a savior has been born to you; he is Christ the Lord. This will be a sign to you: You will find a baby wrapped in cloths in a manger" (Luke 2:10-12).

Scripture taken from, The Young Explorer's Bible, New International Version ® Copyright © 1995 by The Zondervan Corporation and Holy Bible, New International Version®, NIV® Copyright ©1973, 1978, 1984, 2011 by Biblica, Inc.® All Right's Reserved.

Copyright 2020. All rights reserved.

ISBN 978-1-7346873-0-9 (sc)
ISBN 978-1-7346873-1-6 (hc)
ISBN 978-1-7346873-2-3 (ebook)

Dedication

To every person who reads this book, that you may know about Jesus.

When Jake came home from school, Mommy had put out all the Christmas decorations. Of course, she had help from Marty, but she got everything up.

Jake loved all the decorations, but he most loved the Nativity Scene. This decoration was all about Jesus and he'd been learning about Jesus' birth. But he still had many questions.

Mommy saw Jake looking at the Nativity Scene so seriously and she walked over to him.

Jake looked up at her and asked, "Is that God?" pointing to Joseph. "No," Mommy said. "That's Jesus' "bonus" dad, Joseph. God is Jesus' real dad."

"Oh," Jake said, "Why are they with the cows and sheep?" Mommy replied, "There was no room in the Inn."

"Oh, what's an Inn?" Jake asked. Mommy smiled. She knew where this was going and that she just needed to sit down and answer questions. An Inn is like a hotel. There weren't hotels everywhere back then like we have today.

"Oh, but why is baby Jesus in the box that the sheep eat from?" "Well," thought Mommy, "that's called a manger. They didn't have stores to go to at any time of the day to buy baby beds, so they had to use whatever worked. They were pretty smart back then, weren't they, Jake?"

"Oh," Jake said as he thought with a very curious look on his face. "That's why the three wise men had to bring gifts. Right, Mommy?" She replied, "Well, sort of, but I think they brought gifts out of the love in their hearts for Jesus being born and for who He was."

"It's like we give gifts at Christmas out of the love in our hearts to those who mean a lot to us." "Oh," said Jake, "Tell me again, Mommy. Why Jesus was so special, please?"

Mommy went and got the Bible to go along with what she was going to tell Jake. She opened it up to Luke 2:1-20 and showed him where it tells the story of Jesus.

Then she said, "Jake, I want to show you how special Jesus is. You see way back here in the Bible it also told of the Savior coming." She flipped back to Isaiah 7:14 in the Bible and continued. She told him how this verse was written of Jesus long before he came to be born and this is how people knew He was coming and going to be so special.

Mommy read Isiah 7:14, "Therefore the Lord himself will give you a sign: The virgin will be with child and will give birth to a son, and will call him Immanuel."

Jake looked again at the baby Jesus and said, "Oh, I get it. It's like you and dad knew you wanted me before I was born and then when I got here that made me special." Mommy smiled at Jake and said, "Yes, that's real close to the same thing, but Jake, you're special to me, dad and the people that knows us. Jesus is special to everyone, especially everyone who gets to know Him."

Jake gave her a big hug and said, "Thank you, Mommy, I get it now."

Jake went to change his clothes and then he got the mail for Mommy.

It was time for him and Marty to go play.

Later that day Daddy came home and was surprised to see all the wonderful Christmas decorations up. Jake asked if they could read about Jesus birth.

Daddy sat down
with him and Marty
and they read the story
about the Nativity.
Jake made sure
Daddy knew
all the details.

But an angel said to them, "Do not be afraid. I bring you good news of great joy that will be for all the people. Today in the town of David a savior has been born to you; he is Christ the Lord. This will be a sign to you: You will find a baby wrapped in cloths in a manger" (Luke 2:10-12).

Jesus Loves You

A Special Acknowledgement to My Helpers, Jake, Marty, Mommy, and Daddy

www.ingramcontent.com/pod-product-compliance
Lightning Source LLC
Chambersburg PA
CBHW042029100526
44587CB00029B/4349